Contents

KU-092-985

Snowy winter............................4

Icy weather............................6

Keeping warm........................8

Winter fun............................10

Winter sports........................12

On the farm..........................14

Lights and presents...............16

Winter celebrations...............18

Winter animals......................20

Notes for adults....................22

Index...................................24

Snowy winter

brrrr!

Why does it only snow in winter?

Winter

LABURNUM PRESS

Stephen White-Thomson

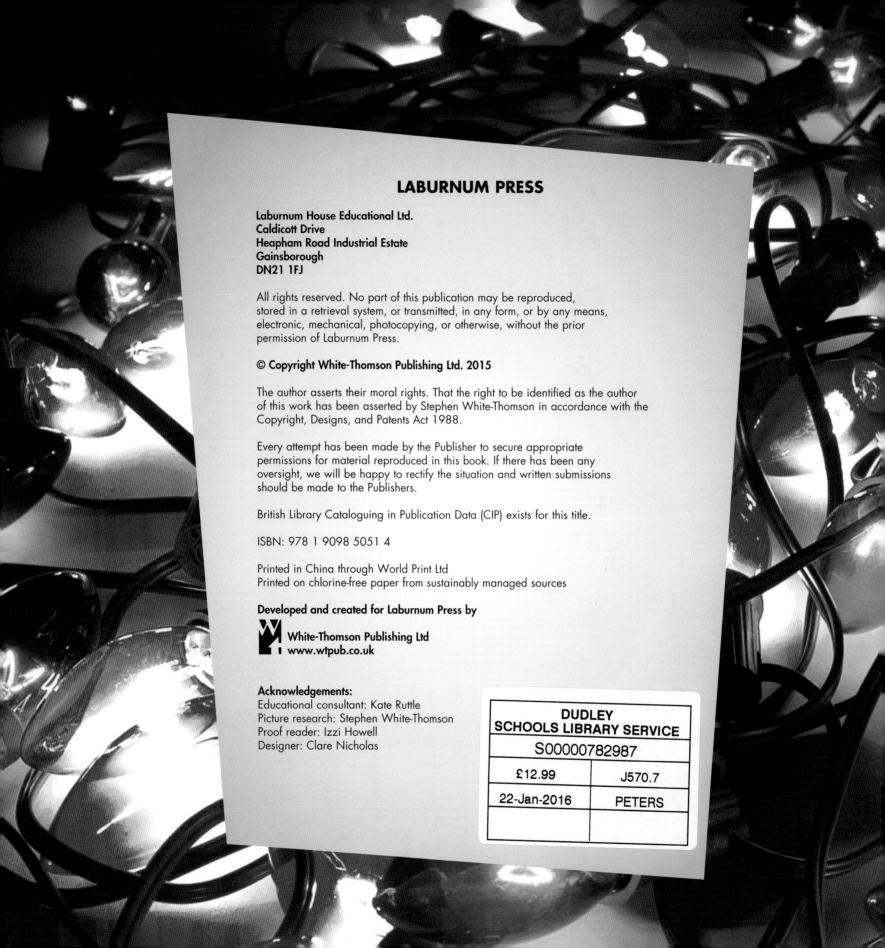

LABURNUM PRESS

Laburnum House Educational Ltd.
Caldicott Drive
Heapham Road Industrial Estate
Gainsborough
DN21 1FJ

British Library Cataloguing in Publication Data (CIP) exists for this title.

ISBN: 978 1 9098 5051 4

Printed in China through World Print Ltd
Printed on chlorine-free paper from sustainably managed sources

Developed and created for Laburnum Press by

White-Thomson Publishing Ltd
www.wtpub.co.uk

Acknowledgements:
Educational consultant: Kate Ruttle
Picture research: Stephen White-Thomson
Proof reader: Izzi Howell
Designer: Clare Nicholas

Machines help us to clear the snow.

whoosh!

Icy weather

What happens to water when it freezes?

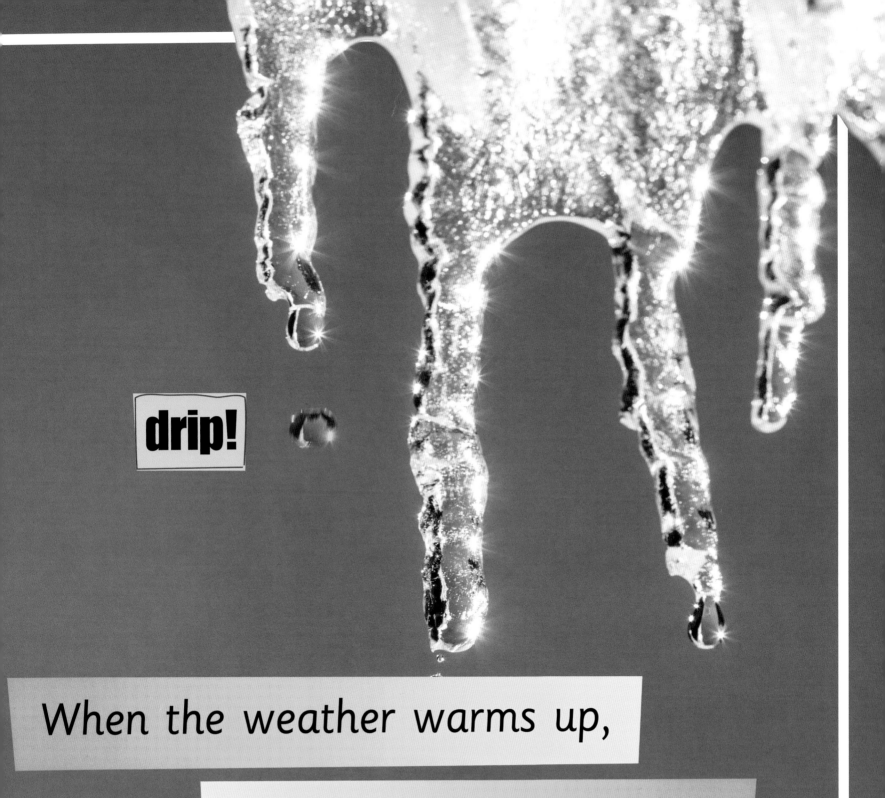

drip!

When the weather warms up,

what happens to the ice?

Keeping warm

When you wear the right clothes, you can stay lovely and warm!

What does a penguin have
instead of clothes?

9

Winter fun

watch out!

Snow can be rolled up

into different shapes.

carrot

It can be made into a snowman!

Winter sports

wheeeeee!

It's fun to slide down snow

on a toboggan or ...

helmet

... on skis.

13

On the farm

When the grass is covered by snow, animals eat hay.

munch! munch!

14

Do you know what these

winter vegetables are called?

Lights and presents

When do you have

fun and presents

in the winter?

Why do people need lights in winter?

menorah

Christmas tree

17

Winter celebrations

fizzbang!

Fireworks explode in the sky on New Year's Eve!

Winter animals

Why do we need to feed birds in the winter?

Some animals sleep all through the winter.

ZZZZZZZ!

Sparklers books are designed to support and extend the learning of young children. Regular winners of Practical Pre-School silver and gold awards, the books' high-interest subjects link to the Early Years curriculum and beyond. Find out more about Early Years foundation stages (EYFS) at www.gov.uk/government/publications/early-years-foundation-stage-framework–2, and reading with children from the National Literacy Trust (www.literacytrust.org.uk).

Themed titles

Winter is one of four **Seasons** titles that encourage children to learn about the fun and informative aspects of their lives in the different seasons. The other titles are **Summer** (ISBN: 978 1 9098 5049 1), **Spring** (ISBN: 978 1 9098 5048 4) and **Autumn** (ISBN: 978 1 9098 5050 7)

The prime areas of learning: (taught in nurseries)

- communication and language
- physical development
- personal, social and emotional development

The specific areas of learning: (taught in reception classes)

- literacy
- mathematics
- understanding the world
- expressive arts and design

Making the most of reading time

When reading with younger children, take time to explore the pictures together. Ask children to find, identify and count or describe different objects. Point out colours and textures. Allow quiet spaces in your reading so that children can ask questions or repeat your words. Try pausing mid-sentence so that children can predict the next word. This sort of participation develops early reading skills.

Follow the words with your finger as you read. The main text is in Infant Sassoon, a clear, friendly font designed for children learning to read and write. The label and sound effects add fun and give the opportunity to distinguish between levels of communication. Where appropriate, labels, sound effects or main text may be presented phonetically. Encourage children to imitate the sounds.

As you read the book, you can also take the opportunity to talk about the book itself with appropriate vocabulary such as "page", "cover", "back", "front", "label" and "page number".

You can also extend children's learning by using the books as a springboard for discussion and further activities. There are a few suggestions on the facing page.

Pages 4–5
Talk about colours that make you feel cold (usually pale blue, greens and yellows). Make a 'cold' collage of colours cut or torn out of catalogues and magazines. Count how many times you see these colours today.

Pages 6–7
Let the children make ice and play with ice-cubes. Challenge them to touch the ice cubes. Can you build a tower of ice cubes? What happens to the cubes? Let the children watch while ice melts. Put a little bit of salt on top of one of the ice cubes. Can the children describe what they see? Use rich language to talk about the ice (e.g. frozen, freeze, melt, sticky, slippery, cold).

Pages 8–9
Find a pile of lost property or spare clothes, including warm coats, winter scarves, boots, summer frocks, shorts. Dress some dolls and teddies to go outside in the winter. What might they need to wear? Will dolls need more clothes or fewer clothes than the furry teddies? Why?

Pages 10–11
Make some pompom snowballs. Cut out two circles of card (about 8-10 cm in diameter) and cut out smaller circles (about the size of a 10p) in the middle. Put your two doughnut-shaped pieces of card together. Show the children how to wind wool around the doughnut shaped pieces of card. Use winter colours. When the hole in the middle is almost full of wool, cut around the edge of the wool until you can see the doughnut pieces. Pull the doughnut pieces of card slightly apart so you can tie a piece of wool tightly around the strings of wool between them. Cut off the card and fluff up your pompom snowballs.

Pages 12–13
Have the children ever been on toboggans, sledges or skis? Let them talk about their experiences. Look at online videos of children enjoying skiing and tobogganing.

Pages 14–15
Bring a selection of winter vegetables. Let the children name them and talk about their colour and shape. Ask the children to draw the vegetables. Display the drawings in a picture of vegetable soup. Make soup from the vegetables and allow the children to taste it.

Pages 16–17
Do the children celebrate during the winter? Christmas, Divali, Hanukkah, Chinese New Year ... other festivals? Ask children to share decorative artefacts and explain what they are for and how they are used in the celebration. Create your own display of celebration artefacts.

Pages 18–19
When the children, the walls and the floor of your setting are well covered, allow them to enjoy splatter painting in firework colours on dark paper. Let them decorate tubes to create 'rockets' and stick these on the firework paintings.

Pages 20–21
Hang a bird feeder on a branch or stick one to a window. Teach the children how to identify some of the birds that come to your feeder. Together, make a pictogram showing how many of each of the kinds of birds come to your feeder.

Index

a
animals 9, 14, 20, 21

b
birds 9, 21

c
Chinese New Year 19
Christmas tree 17
clothes 8, 9

f
farm 14–15
fireworks 18

i
ice 7

l
lights 17

n
New Year's Eve 18

p
presents 16

s
skis 13
snow 4, 5, 10, 12, 14
snowman 11

w
water 6
weather 7
winter sports 12–13

Picture acknowledgements:
Shutterstock: 4 and cover (In Green), 5 (Sergey/Butorin), 8 (Monkey Business Images), 11 (Evgeny Bakharev), 12 (Becky Wass), 14 (Katarzyna Mazurowska), 16 (Gelpi JM), 17 (Frank L Junior) and 17 (inset dvaneh), 18 (melis), 19 (Mariusz S. Jurgielewicz);
Thinkstock: 6 (MaciekG), 7 (Gary Tognoni), 9 (Fuse), 10 (Catherine Yeulet), 13 (hopsalka), 15 (Dimijana), 20 (demarfa), 21 (Dragan Krstic) and 21 (backdrop Wilfinger). Background to 2, 3, 22, 23, 24 is Thinkstock (Ingram Publishing).